SECOND CHANCE

— o —

A COLLECTION OF POETRY

BY

REG JERROM

© Copyright 2004 Reg Jerrom.
All rights reserved. No part of this publication may be reproduced, stored in a retrieval system, or transmitted, in any form or by any means, electronic, mechanical, photocopying, recording, or otherwise, without the written prior permission of the author.

Printed in Victoria, BC, Canada

Note for Librarians: a cataloguing record for this book that includes Dewey Decimal Classification and US Library of Congress numbers is available from the Library and Archives of Canada. The complete cataloguing record can be obtained from their online database at:
www.collectionscanada.ca/amicus/index-e.html
ISBN 1-4120-2664-4

TRAFFORD

This book was published *on-demand* in cooperation with Trafford Publishing. On-demand publishing is a unique process and service of making a book available for retail sale to the public taking advantage of on-demand manufacturing and Internet marketing. On-demand publishing includes promotions, retail sales, manufacturing, order fulfilment, accounting and collecting royalties on behalf of the author.

Offices in Canada, USA, UK, Ireland, and Spain
book sales for North America and international:
Trafford Publishing, 6E–2333 Government St.
Victoria, BC V8T 4P4 CANADA
phone 250 383 6864   toll-free 1 888 232 4444
fax 250 383 6804   email to orders@trafford.com
book sales in Europe:
Trafford Publishing (UK) Ltd., Enterprise House, Wistaston Road Business Centre
Crewe, Cheshire CW2 7RP UNITED KINGDOM
phone 01270 251 396   local rate 0845 230 9601
facsimile 01270 254 983   orders.uk@trafford.com
order online at:
www.trafford.com/robots/04-0492.html

10   9   8   7   6   5   4   3   2

SECOND CHANCE

IN MEMORY OF
MUM & DAD

I dedicate these poems, to my wife and daughter, who have supported and encouraged me through a very difficult period in my life. Their constant love and devotion, has never faltered, enabling me to focus on the future.

INTRODUCTION

— o —

The complexity and structure of life, can often place us in diverse situations, as we journey along, what can at some times be, a very lonely road. Recent unexpected medical problems forced me to re-evaluate my life and make major changes. It is easy to forget how important your life is until you are faced with stark reality.

My priorities changed overnight and I started to realise what the most important aspects of my life were. Possessions, power, wealth, none of these mattered any more. I had suddenly realised that with out your life, you have nothing. John Keats once wrote a poem "I Cry Your Mercy" these four words, constantly echoed in my mind and were my inspiration in writing my book of poetry.

I have always enjoyed reading and writing poetry and I had always said, that one day I would publish my own work. One day, was always the following day. There never seemed to be enough time and my ambition to write and publish, became more and more distant.

When I was forced to re-evaluate my life, I suddenly found, I had the time to devote to my writing, in effect, I had been given a second chance and that is why, the book has been titled second chance.

The poems in this book, cover a wide range of subjects and include love, hope, despair, life, pain, anger and memories. All of which are reflections of my life. There are other topics covered, which include light hearted poems, which I have written from my own imagination. These light hearted poems were written purely for fun, but all have been written from experiences, I have encountered, or seen in the past.

Some of the poems were written at a time, when the main aspect of my life was constant pain, these poems reflect the way I was feeling at the time and the way in which I tried to cope. I have not changed any of the words, from the original hand written version. To do this would alter the concept of the way I was feeling, along with the anger, despair and hope at the time.

Encouragement to write this book has come from family and friends and with there constant support I have been able to achieve my ambition. However sometimes in life we need inspiration. The inspiration for some of my work has come from the beautiful village where I live. The beautiful scenery never ceases to inspire me and constantly reminds me, why I love, this village so much.

I hope you enjoy reading these poems, as much I have enjoyed writing them. They have helped me to understand important values, values which I had neglected. The most important of all, being you own life.

Love can never be measured, Only remembered, valued and treasured.

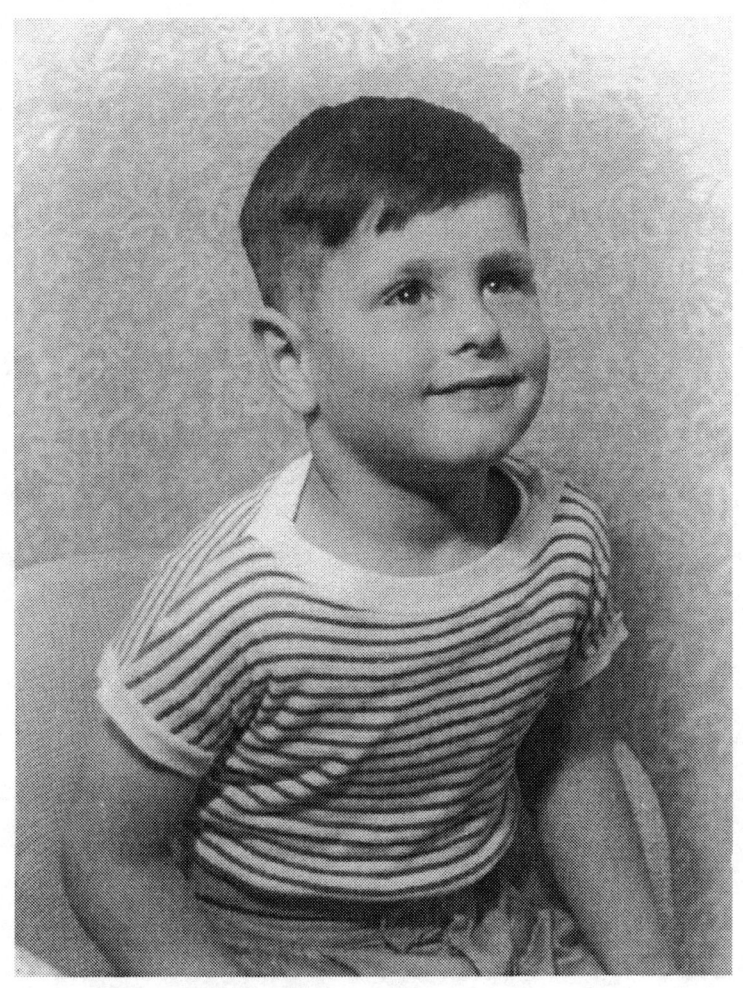

The meaning of life, as yet unknown, But will it be understood, even when fully grown.

Love is given, for us to receive, Your eyes will convey, if this love you deceive.

– CONTENTS –

— o —

INTRODUCTION i
Never In Life 1
I May 2
Those Words 3
Unexplained 4
(A true story told in verse)

SECTION ONE 7
   Boyhood 9
   Father 10
   Mother 11
   Sister 12
   Daughter 13
   Wife 14

SECTION TWO 15
   Love 17
   Passion 18
   Precious Time 19
   Perfect Girl 20
   Bride 21

SECTION THREE 23
   Friendship 25
   New Friends 26
   People 27
   Children 28

SECTION FOUR 29
   Life 31
   Circle Of Life 32
   Trappings Of Life 33
   Breaking Heart 34

– *Contents* –

    Fire 35
    Work 36
    Greed 37

SECTION FIVE 39
    Masquerade 41
    Wounded 42
    Remembering 43
    Twilight Years 44

SECTION SIX 45
    Precious Gift 47
    Mind 48
    Hospital 49
    Positive Mind 50

SECTION SEVEN 51
    Loneliness 53
    Despair 54
    Pain 55
    Frailty 56
    Sleepless Nights 57
    Stressful Life 58
    Homeless 59
    Addicts 60
    Desolation 61
    Unfair 62
    Unexpected 63

SECTION EIGHT 65
    Lord 67
    Faith 68
    Hope 69
    Belief In Yourself 70
    Truth 71

– Contents –

SECTION NINE 73
- Summer 75
- Modern Day Living 76
- Storm 77
- Changes 78
- Sky 79

SECTION TEN 81
- England 83
- The English Garden 84
- The Village 85
- Special Place 86
- England And War 87
- War 88

SECTION ELEVEN 89
- Four Legged Friend 91
- Faithful Friend 92
- Birds 93

SECTION TWELVE 95
Other Topics, Including Light Hearted Poetry
- Theatre 97
- 60's Music 98
- Books 99
- Clock 100
- Regret 101
- Alone 102
- Upper Hand 103
- Nurse 104
- Sheet Music 105
- King And Queen 106
- Time For Tea 107
- Wisdom 108
- Means 109

– *Contents* –

Back 110
Christmas Preparations 111
Christmas Eve 113
Turkey 114
Dream 115
To The End 116

— o —

PICTURES

My parents wedding day
(Picture used with the kind permission of my sisters, Jennifer and Valerie)

Myself as a boy aged five.

Freddie and Nipper,
(Always in my thoughts, if not by my side)

Never In Life

Never in life, give up hope,

There is always someone, to help you cope,

Believe in yourself and what you say,

Look forward, to each bright new day.

– *Second Chance* –

I May

I may not speak, I may not hear,
I may not see, but I still know fear.

I may be young, I may be old,
I may be poor, but I still feel the cold.

I may be happy, I may be sad,
I may be wrong, but I am not mad.

I may struggle each day, I may only just survive,
I may wear a mask, but I thank God I'm alive.

– Second Chance –

Those Words

The words you speak, I love to hear,
Your voice is soft, but crystal clear,
My heart you fill, with love each day,
Oh how I love, those words you say.

— Second Chance —

Unexplained
(A true story told in verse)

For many years, a secret I kept,
Locked firmly away, even when I slept,
A vision, I constantly saw in my mind,
No reasonable explanation, could I find.

At the time I was a boy, just fourteen years old,
Who thought he was a man, big brave and bold,
Outside the day, had now turned to night,
But I was inside, with plenty of light.

I decided to make myself a drink,
Was it tea or coffee, Tea I think,
Our kitchen was big and some what cold,
This part of the house, was very old.

With the cup in my hand, I approached the door to the hall,
A long narrow passage, but very tall,
What happened next, still makes me go cold,
Before me a woman in black, small and old.

Her hair was grey, pulled back from her face,
The collar of her dress, looked like lace,
Only briefly, did I see her there,
Before she disappeared, gone but where.

I did not move, I was frightened you see,
In my hand, I still held my cup of tea,
Slowly I walked back, to the kitchen sink,
Placed my cup in the bowl and tried to think.

What had I seen, or thought I had seen,
A trick of the light, it might have been,
Back at the door, I looked again along the hall,
There was no one there, just the hallway narrow and tall.

— Second Chance —

I decided at once, that I would run,
Back to the front room, as this was no fun,
The door I closed as quick, as could be,
Not once did I look behind, for fear of what I might see.

I sat on the couch and starred at the door,
Shaking and sweating, like I had never experienced before,
My parents returned and shouted to me,
I was relieved, happy, full of glee.

This secret I kept, for many long years,
A constant reminder, of those terrible fears,
Then one day, the old mantle clock went wrong,
And I found out, to whom it used to belong.

I was told of a woman, who had once lived here,
A gentle old sole, very kind and very dear,
At this point, I let my secret unfold,
As my story I knew, could now be told.

My mother listened intensely and nodded her head,
At all I had explained and said,
She will do you no harm, she will do you no wrong,
For some reason here, is where she feels she does belong.

Was it a ghost, who can say,
But I still remember that day,
The lady in black, I never again did meet,
Even though she died, in the room where I used to sleep.

SECTION ONE

BOYHOOD

Gone those carefree days, I once did enjoy,
When I was a child just a boy,
Days spent at school, games played in the field,
Swords made of cardboard, as was the shield,
Cricket and football, played with friends,
Tee shirts and shorts, no expensive trends,
Pocket money you earned, upon completion of a task,
No extra was available, you did not even ask,
A picnic in the field,
Jam sandwich and squash, would be your yield,
Bicycles ridden round and about,
Laughter rang out with the occasional loud shout,
Polite and courteous, showing the utmost respect,
To people of all ages and intellect,
Angels we were not, trouble we could find,
Not getting caught, always on our mind,
Parents always strict but fair,
Their love individual, given as a pair,
Home always neat and tidy,
Everything in place, a boiler or grate supplied the heat,
Food lovingly prepared, laid out on the table,
Meals eaten together, if we were able,
Conversations after dinner, a routine everyday,
Eagerly awaited, always lots to hear and say,
When bedtime came, no arguments were heard,
You went straight away, without a word,
Carefree days sheltered from the worries of life,
Protected by parents, two people a husband and wife.

– Second Chance –

FATHER

A son looks up to his father to admire,
The home he's built, there own small empire,
The love between them, there to see,
Standing tall, like a magnificent chestnut tree,
Time together, becomes memories to cherish,
Even though they may disagree, each others company they relish,
The son soon grows, they become two men together,
Blood and love will bond them forever,
The time will arrive, when the son will leave,
A new life to start, possibly a family to conceive,
Wisdom, knowledge and love taken, as you go away,
These gifts freely given, with you will always stay.

– Second Chance –

MOTHER

How can I ever repay,
What you have given me, this and every day,
My life, your love, everything I am,
From my birth to being pushed in my pram,
You picked me up, wiped away my tears,
Held me in your arms, took away my fears,
Your love was endless, always more in store,
This like a shield I wore,
As I grew I caused you pain,
Witnessed you crying, outside in the rain,
You had not failed, it was me,
I let you down, at the time I did not see,
Your love for me never faltered,
From my birth, it never altered,
You cared for me, always gave me a smile,
Defended me, in your own unique style,
Laid awake in your bed at night,
Until I was home, back in your sight,
Advice you gave with a gentle guiding hand,
No matter where I was, in what ever land,
You never judged me, in all the years that I was growing,
Your love always there, always showing,
Dear mother my love for you is straight from my heart,
A love from the moment of my birth did start,
I will love and defend you until my last breath,
This love cannot cease, even in death.

SISTER

Sister, so gentle, so kind,
Not afraid to speak your mind
Never far away,
Always in my life to stay,

A shoulder to cry on, in time of need,
Kindness shown in word and deed,
Childhood memories to share,
Of times gone by, for which we care,

Blood the family tie, always carried,
Even if you are married,
Laughter and tears shared, in times good and bad,
Situations remembered, some happy, some sad,

Words, gestures, perhaps a small token,
Enforce a love, never to be broken,
A unique bond between sister and brother,
Given to us, by our father and mother.

— Second Chance —

DAUGHTER

When first my eyes beheld the miracle of your birth,
I stood and cried, I had no worth,
This helpless baby, I helped to conceive,
I promised that you, I would never deceive,
From that day on I dedicated my life to you,
To be a part of everything you wanted to do,
My love for you, always repaid,
In the things you do and say, items that you, for me, have made,
All through the years that you were growing,
Our love became a bond, never hidden always showing,
Now grown you have become a beautiful lady,
One day this love you will understand, with your own baby,
You were conceived in love, of which you are a true reflection,
Through my eyes you are and always will be, perfect perfection.

WIFE

My darling, to me you are divine,
Delicate skin, so soft, so fine,
Your body a temple, I worship each day,
Sometimes in silence, if there are no words to say,
Your eyes covey the love, you carry in your heart,
Of which I pray, I am one small part,
Your face I see in my sleep,
From the love I hold for you, in my heart, way down deep,
The ground on which you walk, should be showered in gold,
This world should be told, of the love for you I hold,
When we are apart, I yearn for your touch,
The words you speak, I miss so much,
Angels in heaven, must surely sing your praise,
Angelic tones in harmony, their voices raise,
Singing of the love, we share together,
Joyous that we will be one, forever.

SECTION TWO

LOVE

The touch of your hand, the smile of your face,
Images of sensuous fine lace,
Two people together, bonded by the heart,
There for each other, never to be apart,
Hands that gently, caress each arm.
Lips pressed together, so peaceful, so calm,
Eyes that convey, all there is to say,
A loving embrace, given in a special way,
Bodies as one, in perfect harmony,
Sharing a glass, of fine chardonnay,
Touching and feeling, each moment a pleasure,
There for both, to cherish and treasure,
Embracing each other, two people together,
A romantic, peaceful true love for ever.

– Second Chance –

PASSION

Passion burns, deep inside,
Engulfing your body, forming no divide,
Man relentless in his desire,
Fulfillment is what, he doth require.

Women, more complex, than there male counterpart,
There passion intense, more from the heart,
Love not always, can you acquire,
But women must also, fulfill there desire.

Man can be gentle and kind,
When a woman, is all he has on his mind,
Desire and passion, both can enjoy,
Natural feelings, that no lives destroy.

— Second Chance —

PRECIOUS TIME

This precious time, we are allowed to share,
Should be filled with, love compassion and care,
Will I ever say, all I have to say,
Will I value and treasure, each new day.

What if tomorrow, never came,
Could life, ever be the same,
How would I manage, without you by my side,
The one in whom, I always confide.

In my mind, I know this day will arrive,
Which one of us will be left, alone to survive,
Together we are strong, alone, just weak,
Each others love in life, is all we seek.

Each day is a gift, for us to live,
Our love to each other, we freely give,
But which one of us, will be left to cry,
Walking alone, under a clear blue sky.

— Second Chance —

PERFECT GIRL

I will love you every day,
I will love you come what may,
I do not care what people say,
I will love you every day.

More and more, I think of you,
No matter what I do,
Every where I see your face,
To my heart, you have won the race.

I will give you anything,
Clothes and pearls, a diamond ring,
There is no way you will ever know,
Just how much I love you so.

Please do not make a fool of me,
I love you so, it's plain to see,
All my life, I dreamed I'd find,
The perfect girl, from my mind.

Will you give me your love so sweet,
So our lips at last can meet,
Is this love about to start,
Or will we, just stay apart.

Now I have said, what I had to say,
I must listen come what may,
Feelings that I store inside,
There for you, if you decide.

– Second Chance –

BRIDE

Final preparations all complete,
Guests arriving, family and friends they will meet,
This day once a dream, so distant,
Now here without, any resistance,
Excited and nervous, the bride prepares in her room,
Thoughts in her mind, of the man she will wed this afternoon,
Her dress cascades down the wall,
Reflecting the light, shimmering like a clear water fall,
Collecting like a pool, on the blue carpeted floor,
Gently the breeze, blows the vale across the door,
Across the flowers, so fragrant and bright,
Next to the door on the right,
Helpers in attendance, preparing and sharing,
Items of clothing, some rather daring,
Once dressed they will help the bride,
Slide into her gown, gently to guide,
Her veil and train, delicate and fine,
White satin shoes, complete the line,
Fast approaching the time when they must depart,
Vows to make, never again to be apart,
The bride emerges, perfection in white,
This day the start of a new life,
When two become one, as man and wife.

SECTION THREE

FRIENDSHIP

A true friend, someone who is always there,
Someone to call on, no matter when or where,
A person there for you in time of need,
Even though there advice, you do not always heed.

A true friend, with whom you spend such happy day's,
Enjoying life, in a variety of different way's,
Someone to confide in, in times of woe,
This person you love and respect so.

A true friend, will give a shoulder to cry upon,
Wipe your tears, give you the confidence to go on,
Sharing the good times, crying with laughter,
Remembering these times long after.

A true friend, so hard to find,
Once found, always with you in your mind,
Cherish this person, of whom you are so fond,
You are truly blessed, to have such a unique bond.

– Second Chance –

NEW FRIENDS

Abroad in the sun, new people you meet,
Enjoying themselves, in the glorious heat,
Strangers at first, friends then became,
Life styles not always, need be the same,
Outings together can last late into the night,
In bars talking by flickering candle light,
Days on the beach, or by the pool,
A parasol used to keep you cool,
Meals together in perfect day light,
Under the clear blue sky, no clouds in sight,
The holiday all too soon is over,
Home you must go, possibly over the white cliffs of Dover,
Addresses exchanged, as a parting gift,
Sadness is felt, photographs can give you a lift,
All promise to write, without fail,
Can this friendship survive, by phone, post and e-mail.

― *Second Chance* ―

PEOPLE

People pass each other in the street,
Hurrying to an appointment, someone to meet,
Each one an individual in their own right,
Conducting their business by day or night,
Time both there enemy and there friend,
Dictating how long they have to spend,
Work and leisure, once separate, now seem combined,
Lives more complicated, less defined,
Technology evolves at an alarming pace,
More time to find, just to stay in the race,
Pressure now part, of our lives every day,
Stress the price we have to pay,
Gone the time of the carefree days,
We have adapted to new and complicated ways,
Our lives completely turned around,
A new way of living and thinking has been found,
Progression a step you have to take,
Scarifies you may have to make,
Companies crave profit, this is there only concern,
Money for them you are there to earn,
Loyalty once so highly regarded,
Now so easily discarded,
Life is so important, stand back and see,
The person you would really like to be.

– Second Chance –

CHILDREN

Children laughing as they play,
So much they have to say,
Innocent faces with smiles abound,
As you look around,
Studies soon they will attend,
Learning from lessons and games, like make pretend,
Oblivious there paths will take in the future,
Learning from parents, teachers perhaps a tutor,
All with seeds of knowledge, ready to be sown,
In eager minds to be nurtured and grown,
So much they have to learn,
In future years they must earn,
Innocent faces all too soon disappear,
The right direction for them, you must steer,
But listen and learn, from what children have to say,
They have no pre-conceptions clouding their way.

SECTION FOUR

LIFE

Many things are needed to survive,
Food and water alone, is not enough to remain alive,
Clothes protect us from the cold,
Heat required for all, young and old,
Doctors to turn to in time of need,
Advice they give, not always do we heed,
Work a place we sell our skills,
Exchanged for money, used for food and bills,
Homes our refuge, a place we cherish,
Possessions we own, ours to relish,
Society judges you, on your chosen career,
Earning capacity, make that crystal clear,
Class distinction, still with us today,
Never will go away, here to stay,
Money and wealth, a natural desire,
To this, people try to aspire,
Perhaps we should stand and reflect,
On our way of life, its effect,
The world, a fragile place,
Home to every creed, colour and race,
Our bodies one day we will leave,
Un aware the greatest wealth we had was the air we had to breath.

CIRCLE OF LIFE

Throughout time, in every nation and race,
Time is precious, as we struggle to keep up with life's pace,
Opportunities, there for all to acquire,
Even though, we do not always obtain our hearts desire.

This world, a wonderful place to explore,
Obtaining memories, for your mind to store,
Pictures convey instant memories, that may bring a smile,
Of times you remember, possibly not for a while.

One of the greatest moments in life,
The birth of a child, from a partner or wife,
The greatest gift any woman can bestow,
As a man this will make you humble and low.

The circle of life is complex and long,
In proceeding we may sometimes go wrong,
Search and look deep with in your heart,
Remember your memories, this is your life, if only one small part.

– Second Chance –

TRAPPINGS OF LIFE

Love once colourful and bright,
Now a distant memory, gone from sight,
Days together, in the sun,
Two people as one.

Carefree times, relaxing as time passed by,
Walking through fields, under the sky,
Money there was none, each other our only need,
Idyllic days, of happiness, not greed.

Laughter once loud, now silence, no sound,
Love that once conquered all, now turned around,
Two people once lovers,
Now strangers beneath the covers.

Words spoken with warmth, now conveyed so cold,
Two lives in pieces, nothing left to hold,
Different directions, have been taken,
Each other now forsaken.

Happiness, once the most treasured possession,
Greed must now be our confession,
Carefree days, replaced by meetings and fashionable bars,
Working long hours, for fast expensive cars.

The trappings of life, so hard to ignore,
Once tasted, you hunger for more,
Love can become fragile and week,
As power, position and money you seek.

– Second Chance –

BREAKING HEART

Tell me where did we go wrong,
Both of us thought, we were strong,
There was no way we could foresee,
What the future would be.

The love we shared, grew from a seed,
Fulfilled our lives and our need,
We made a vow, we would not part,
To each we gave our heart.

Was it you, or was it me,
Who was blind and did not see,
The road ahead that was our destiny,
Was nothing more than a mystery.

My days are long and covered with a haze,
I live my life, as though I'm in a maze,
I loved you so, I know you loved me too,
What now, am I to do.

I gave you all the love, I had to give,
Our whole lives through, I thought that we would live,
Now every day, I wake up on my own,
In this one room, I now call home.

A brand new love, I know that you have found,
Your roots, now firmly planted in the ground,
This love of ours, now finally at it's end,
My breaking heart, I must now mend.

– Second Chance –

FIRE

Home our refuge, safe and secure,
Holding for us this magnetic lure,
Warm and inviting, peaceful and calm,
These four walls keep you from harm.

Dangers exist, of which we must be aware,
Tasks under taken, sometimes with out care,
Time the factor, not the cause,
Sometimes we must stop and pause.

Magnificent and powerful, with colours aglow,
Burning brightly, performing its own little show,
Fire for warmth, contained by a guard,
Should be respected with the highest regard.

Candles that flicker, a soft glowing light,
Must never be left alone, by day or night,
Cookers will provide, our favourite delight,
Must be respected, once alight.

Fire can cause, much misery and harm,
Every home should have a smoke alarm,
Close doors firmly at the end of the day,
As off to bed you make your way.

Flames engulf homes, burning at will,
Acrid smoke, fills every crevice, covers every sill,
Your family and home you must protect,
Treat any cause of fire, with the greatest respect.

– Second Chance –

WORK

Eyes wide open, suddenly awake,
Out of bed, your way you must make,
Time the key, which rules your day,
With you every step of the way.

Traffic congestion, found in every town and city,
People in a hurry, show little compassion or pity,
Pollution encountered, where ever you are,
Traveling by foot, in trains, cab or car.

Laptops and mobiles, essential for all,
Eagerly waiting, for that all important message or call,
Meetings the place you strive to shine,
Though it may be the cause, of others decline.

Sentiment and loyalty, no where to be found,
Danger lurks, all around,
Projects to complete and present on time,
Lateness not tolerated, the ultimate crime.

Hours that once were nine to five,
No longer exist, if you wish to survive,
Lives you once could plan and arrange,
Now un-predictable, always subject to change.

– Second Chance –

GREED

The news we watch, broadcast all day,
Pictures and words, from far away,
Scenes that sometimes we wish we had not scene,
Misery, poverty, war and destruction, shown in our homes so clean,
Children crying, some to ill even to cry,
Parents in despair, asking, screaming why,
Hospitals at breaking point, unable to cope,
Some people just stare, they have given up all hope,
This world supplies our every need,
Most countries only concerned with there own greed,
Money, power and domination, the issue to resolve,
For a world of peace, in harmony to revolve.

SECTION FIVE

MASQUERADE

I've seen right through, your fancy masquerade,
As each day before me, you parade,
Gone those days, when I was blind,
The truth ignored, from deep in my mind.

I once believed, those words you spoke,
But those same words, my heart have broke,
No words can repair, this life torn apart,
Now is the time, to make a new start.

There was no one, in whom I could confide,
My loneliness and despair, hidden deep inside,
The tears I cried, I'll cry no more,
Over your fancy masquerade and you, who I now deplore.

– Second Chance –

WOUNDED

Where did you go, when you left my side,
Walked out of my life, stole my pride,
Where did you find, a place to hide,
A place to shelter, from my side.

You left me in, the cold and rain,
Ensured my agony and pain,
You showed no feelings, as you walked away,
I never had the chance, to ask you to stay.

You wounded me, like I had never known,
Left my heart bleeding, left me all alone,
You took my life, then threw it away,
Left me in pieces, to face each day.

You broke my heart, shattered my pride,
I felt as though, I had died,
But now each day, I feel so alive,
With you no longer, by my side.

— Second Chance —

REMEMBERING

Life is full of so much pleasure,
Times to cherish and treasure,
Holidays abroad, for which you have saved so long,
Listening to your favourite song,
The eagerly awaited birth of a child,
Relaxing outside, when the weather is sunny and mild,
Perhaps a wedding, for you to attend,
Playing simple games, like make pretend,
These things and many more,
There for your mind, to remember and store,
No one can predict, what the future may hold,
But your memories remain, stories that can be told,
Future generations, will listen in admiration,
Of your personal memories, through your words and communication.

– Second Chance –

TWILIGHT YEARS

Where oh where, has my life disappeared,
This time now come, which I have feared,
Youthful years gone, now I just survive,
Once so young and alive,
Wasted portions of life, planted in my mind,
Days long gone, so far behind,
Happiness now no more than a distant dream,
Remembering times, laying by a silent stream,
Dreams and ambitions, some how slipped slowly by,
I have no explanations, even though I ask myself why,
Now in my twilight years,
The time long gone for tears,
Generations to come, hold the future of our land,
Their lives they carry in the palm of their hand,
Possibilities in life abound, on a road long and wide,
Opportunities for those who do not hide,
How many will be, like I am this day,
Wondering how, they lost their way.

SECTION SIX

PRECIOUS GIFT

Life the most precious gift, you can receive,
In yourself, you must believe,
Your destiny you carve, over many long years,
Building your future, conquering your fears.

Situations will occur, you never expected,
Problems that can go, un-detected,
Your health, you take for granted every day,
In seconds, can be taken away.

The tapestry of life, is rich and bold,
There for all, to acquire and hold,
Enjoy your life, as you journey along the way,
One day it will end, in this you have no say.

– Second Chance –

MIND

Alert and complex minds, plan our destiny,
Believing in yourself, requires great intensity,
Ideas in mind for the life you require,
Each day closer to your hearts desire,
Situations of which you have no control,
A time needed for all your resolve,
Health taken for granted, by day and night,
More important issues, come first in our sight,
This life, for which we thirst,
Surely means we should put our health first,
Why then do we tend to dismiss or ignore,
Signs that a doctor may need to explore,
Money stature and wealth,
Is this our requirement, over our health.

— Second Chance —

HOSPITAL

Words like DNA, are carried in your heart,
Conveying your feelings, if only one small part,
Expressions are used by all everyday,
Each in their own individual way,

Life can be cruel, catch you off guard,
Sometimes you listen to words you find so hard,
A simple consultation can send your mind in turmoil, become confused,
These words you hear are true, even though your mind tries to refuse,

Medical staff will attend you day and night,
In hospital you are always in there sight,
With cheer there tasks they duly perform,
Diligence and duty, to which they all conform,

The back bone of Britain, these people truly are,
They are our health service, each and every one a star,
So with my hand placed firmly on my heart,
I praise you all for playing your part.

— Second Chance —

POSITIVE MIND

Days stretched out before you, long and dark,
The outlook, bleak and stark,
Before your eyes, there stands a solid brick wall,
Dark, desolate and tall.

Once where shadows were cast, now you see desolation,
All roads and avenues, lead only to desperation,
Physical strength, once abundant,
Now completely redundant.

Drugs help and ease the pain,
As each day your life, you try and regain,
Determination your only weapon, with which to fight,
As you struggle through each day and night.

Independence gone, now others help you cope,
Each day the same, so you pray and hope,
Suddenly in your mind, you see a glimmer of light,
A way to proceed, could your future, now be bright,

No one can hold you back,
Confidence you have, even if strength, you lack,
Now focused with all the determination, you can acquire,
To reach this light, your goal, your hearts desire.

SECTION SEVEN

LONELINESS

Sitting at his window all alone,
A solitary figure, face grey like stone,
Watching as the world slowly goes by,
There all alone, sometimes he may cry.

Sitting at his window, curtains dirty and torn,
His favourite chair, old and well worn,
Feet on a carpet, thread bare, nearly bold,
This is his room, un-inviting and cold.

Sitting at his window, watching people in the street,
Standing by houses, all tidy and neat,
Talking to each other, they pass the time of day,
Before they go off, on their way.

Sitting at his window, hoping someone may nod there head,
A gesture where no words need to be said,
One day perhaps, he may have a visitor,
Someone to talk to, possibly the minister.

Sitting at his window, is where he used to be,
Looking out for all to see,
Did any one notice he used to be there,
This lonely old man, gone no more to stare.

– Second Chance –

DESPAIR

In the depths of despair,
Your mind fights hard to repair,
Thoughts of which you cannot tell,
Gone the days when you were healthy and well.

Darkness forms a barrier from all,
Standing before you, like a solid brick wall,
Help needed to conquer your fear,
Of life's new path, of which you are not clear.

To ask for help is not a weakness,
It is a ray of light, within your bleakness,
To stay in the dark, only your self you deceive,
Open your heart, for help to receive.

Life once embraced full on,
Still there for you, not gone,
The answer will lye, deep within,
Ask for help, never give in.

— Second Chance —

PAIN

Pain is a gift, or so I was told,
From a dear old lady, a true sight to behold,
Her face all aglow, as she sat in her chair,
Telling her stories, with her shinning white hair.

Pain is a gift, I still hear her say,
One I must live with, each and every day,
Never complaining, as she chatted away,
Just grateful you came for a short stay.

Pain is a gift, now older I understand,
Words of wisdom, just simple, not grand,
A gift that is given to all in the land,
There with you forever, no matter what you have planned.

Pain is a gift, part of every day life,
Sometimes severe, it cuts likes a knife,
You struggle to cope, so easy to give in,
Your smile disappears, replaced by a grin.

Pain is a gift, one for which I did not ask,
Problems occur with even the smallest task,
Each day seems so long, as they slowly pass by,
This gift we were given, but why.

FRAILTY

Complex and intricate, the human body is a wonder,
Like natures rain, wind, snow and thunder,
Life taken so much for granted,
Delicate minds where the seed of life is planted,
The world offers so much to explore,
Scenes of beauty, but also destruction we deplore,
Mans greed, where ever you look,
Written in documents, sometimes in a book,
Man and woman aspire to achieve their aspirations,
Sometimes revealing hidden revelations,
Tragic events, fill our world every day,
Where nature and man compete in each and every way,
Only one force will stay and stand tall,
Mans ultimate frailty, his final downfall.

— Second Chance —

SLEEPLESS NIGHTS

Sitting alone in the still of the night,
Artificial light glows softly, but bright,
The house so quiet as others still sleep,
This lonely existence, I long not to keep.

Time my enemy, as at the clock I look,
Pausing for a while, whilst reading my book,
Soon the dawn will arrive, the household will come alive
This sleepless night will cease, my spirits will then revive.

STRESSFUL LIFE

Complicated and stressful, the life of a doctor or nurse,
This profession of there's, sometimes a curse,
Caring for the sick and those in need,
Commitment required, not greed,
Working to resolve problems and complications,
Through their faces, you see there dedication,
Strenuous routines are the norm,
Administered from dusk through to morn,
These people we take so much for granted,
Always there in our minds, from birth this seed was planted,
In times of need, they are there our own professional fighting cavalry,
There courageous endeavors respected, except in there salary,
Praise and admiration, should come from us all,
To those caring, professional people, who have answered the call.

— Second Chance —

HOMELESS

Another day looms, offering nothing but doom,
Eyes now wide open, show only gloom,
Barely existing, no desire little hope,
Trying so hard, just to cope.

Another days looms, possessions you pack,
In carrier bags, perhaps an old sack,
This doorway you slept in, now time to vacate,
As busy people, it will soon accommodate.

Another day looms, as you walk away,
Looking for somewhere, to spend your day,
Begging the only way you can survive,
Money for food, your spirit to revive.

Another day looms, time has no meaning,
A welcome escape, if you start dreaming,
Some people throw coins into your hat,
Directly in front of where you are sat.

Another day looms, move or be moved,
Verbal abuse, your dignity long ago removed,
Clothes all dirty, ripped and torn,
You have nothing else, that can be worn.

Another day looms, slowly you walk away,
Looking for somewhere, this night you can stay,
The money you begged, perhaps a bottle you will buy,
Your past you remember, sometimes you may cry.

— Second Chance —

ADDICTS

Addicts revolve around there next fix,
Lethal concoctions, sometimes they mix,
Money they always seem to acquire,
To feed this addiction, this desire,
Most to society have nothing left to give,
In squalor and filth most will live,
Drugs once tried, for an experiment or dare,
Have produced addicts with little or no care,
Suppliers get rich, inflicting misery and harm,
Compassion they have none, even though they may use their charm,
Society the ones who suffer most,
Through out the land on every coast,
Shoplifting and burglary, the most common of crime,
Addicts may try from time to time,
Campaigns and posters hold nothing back,
Showing what can happen, with drugs like crack,
Doctors help and so do the clinics,
Even though there are many cynics,
A world wide problem, with yet no answer,
Illegal drugs, a malignant cancer.

– Second Chance –

DESOLATION

Desolate days,
My life I live in a haze,
What will my future be,
I look, but cannot see.

My eyes see clouds, in my mind,
No ray of hope there, for me to find,
Another endless day,
There must be another way.

How did I let this, happen to me,
I closed my mind, so I would not see,
I am the cause, I was wrong,
Where now, do I belong.

My life, is a constant strain,
Each day, filled with pain,
My health, I choose to ignore,
As I have, many times before.

Can this nightmare, I survive,
Will my spirit, ever revive,
No one can help me, in this fight,
I must battle on, with all my might.

– Second Chance –

UNFAIR

I watch plants, grow from seed,
Water is all they need,
Perfect formations, they display,
Gently swaying, they appear to play.

Why then, is my life so unfair,
Bringing me, to the edge of despair,
Is this my penance, for being born,
My life in ruins, all shattered and torn.

No one is to blame, only me,
All the signs were there, for me to see,
But I ignored them, the job came first,
This incasable, hunger and thirst.

Working to ensure, the company expanded,
All your energy, was expected and demanded,
But in my time of need, they were not there,
Doors firmly closed, they did not care.

Incapacity means, you do not comply,
As on you, they can no longer rely,
Another person, soon fills your position,
Profit there only concern, there only mission.

If only life were as simple, as that of a plant,
This wish in my mind, I would grant,
That there would be, no more tears for me to cry,
Once grown and flowered, I would die.

– Second Chance –

UNEXPECTED

The sun shines bright, this glorious day,
People hurry, as they make there way,
I watch with envy and remember that used to be me,
Part of society and proud so to be,
My future, hardly crossed my mind,
Now explanations, are hard to find,
Should I have planned, for the unexpected,
My health, I now know I neglected,
But people are there and they are kind,
With words and gestures, by my side when I have cried,
No one can understand, the way I feel,
In time, perhaps I will heel,
But I will survive, so I must be strong,
Even though, the road ahead is dark and long.

In my mind, I often despair,
That my broken life, will never repair,
These thoughts, I must confess,
Cause me heartache and distress,
There is no need, for me to be on my own,
I can always, talk to someone on the phone,
Life does not always go, according to plan,
For either woman, or man,
But life is the greatest gift, we ever receive,
So in myself, I must believe,
Each day I know, a little further I will proceed,
I am determined, I will not concede,
With help, this fight I know I can win,
But why oh why, did I ever let this begin.

SECTION EIGHT

LORD

Lord, your help I often ask,
To complete even the smallest task,
You are the one to whom I can always turn,
In this life, of which I have so much to learn.

Life changes each and every day,
People rule your life with what they do and say,
We have learned to adapt, in order to survive,
In this demanding world, vast and alive.

The bible gives us your teaching,
Words that can be heard in sermon and preaching,
The true path of life, is there if we look,
Through the pages of the holy book.

– Second Chance –

FAITH

Religion your faith, your own belief,
There for you, in times of grief,
A place of sanctuary, a place to pray,
Guidance you seek, along life's lonely way,
A belief you can carry, at work or home,
Prejudices sometimes you have to overcome,
Faith a choice, not chosen by all,
Dedicated lives for some, who answer the call,
Teachings and sermons, lengthy, always holy,
Aspects of religion, fully taught, but slowly,
Icons, statues and stained glass tell a story,
Of your chosen religion in all its glory,
A simple wooden cross, preferred by some,
Conveys a message to all who come,
Personal belief, is carried in your heart,
Thought of and studied like art,
Believers may not always to church attend,
Hidden beliefs, they may not always defend,
The right to believe, or not, as individual as each human being,
Not through the eyes of what some body else is seeing.

– Second Chance –

HOPE

Never in life give up hope,
There is always someone, who can help you cope,
Despair so dark, you cannot see,
The person you are, the person you could be,
Help is there, reach out your hand,
Where ever you are, in which ever land,
Darkness you carry in your mind,
Can be lifted, the right key you must find,
Trust in others, listen to what they say,
They can help you find the key, show you another way,
Life can be bright, full of pleasure,
Future years, there for you to treasure,
There is always a way, to change the darkness you hide inside,
Believe in yourself, lift this darkness, you strive so hard to hide.

— *Second Chance* —

BELIEF IN YOURSELF

Where were you, when I needed a friend,
In whom I could confide and depend,
I bared my soul, that lonely day,
Praying you would hear, what I had to say,
The words I spoke, were harsh and strong,
Looking back, I now know I was wrong,
I needed a sign, to guide me along,
To help me survive and remain strong,
But even though, my tears were real,
I saw no sign, your presence I did not feel,
Confused and alone, as day turned to night,
In the dark I sat, without any light,
There was no one now, in whom I could confide,
Nobody there, by my side,
I searched for the answers, in my mind,
The strength for this task, hard to find,
But focused, I now saw a glimmer of light,
That rapidly grew and burned so bright,
You had not deserted me, you were there all along,
I had pushed you away, forgive me, I was wrong.

– Second Chance –

TRUTH

Secrets we hide in cupboards locked fast,
Deep in our minds, to bury the past,
Some so black, we try to forget,
Things once done, we so now regret,
Success a goal, we strive to achieve,
Even if others we have to deceive,
Enemies made along the way,
May delve into your past each and every day,
Slowly your past, will always hunt you down,
Defenses will fall, no smile now, only a frown,
Truth a mighty weapon, that cannot be broken,
Facts written on paper, words that are spoken,
This we do each and every day,
Today is tomorrows past, ensure you are not made to pay.

SECTION NINE

SUMMER

Summer thou art finally here,
Bringing my heart so much cheer,
Winter days now passed,
Shadows, no longer you cast.

Brightness replaces winters gloom,
Golden rays enter every room,
Natural warmth, can now be found,
Echoed in light and sound.

Nature now so alive,
Animals appear, who the winter did survive,
Flowers in abundance, fragrance so delicate,
Perfume the air, with a scent so intricate.

A new found freedom, to be enjoyed by all,
No longer confined by wood, or bricks that form a wall,
Outside a space now in your agenda,
Vast and magnificent, there in all its splendor.

MODERN DAY LIVING

Winters that once were long and cold,
Now shorter and warmer, from those days of old,
Global warming has had this effect,
Modern day living, the cause of this defect,
Floods that happened, once in a while,
Now furious and frequent, covering mile after mile,
Damage and destruction, inflicted along the way,
Devastation visible by the light of day,
No country now safe from nature's aggression,
Fuelled by man in his vocation and profession.

– Second Chance –

STORM

The howling wind, an eerie sound,
Engulfing everything, fiercely blowing around,
Trees bend, branches can be heard falling,
On to roads, places where people go walking,
Rain is blown in every direction,
Crashing onto windows, into your reflection,
Roofs on sheds, holding on, barely there,
Felt ripped off, gone, but where,
Streets almost deserted, only a few brave the storm,
Most people at home, in the warm,
Cars drive slowly, wipers moving so fast,
Roads resemble rivers, wide and vast,
Debris blows by, then out of sight,
Gone we know not where, on this dreadful night.

— Second Chance —

CHANGES

Leaves once green, now brown, russet and gold,
Swaying in the wind, soon to fall in this weather so cold,
Autumn when nature changes so fast,
Seeds of winter now being cast,
Open doors in homes, now closed tight,
Days quickly mingle into night,
Fires replace the suns warm rays,
This the beginning of cold, dark, damp days,
Nature during this time will sleep,
Until spring when bulbs through soil will peep,
Colours fresh and bright on flowers appear,
Brighter longer days, signal a new time of year,
Out door pursuits regenerated with gusto and pace,
This time of year welcomed by the human race.

– Second Chance –

SKY

Looking at the clear blue sky,
Slowly it moves, way up high,
Perhaps a cloud may come your way,
But nothing there will spoil your day.

Clouds in white, with shades of grey,
Moving along, not here to stay,
Shapes they form, in different guises,
Large and small, all various sizes.

The sun shines brightly, its rays so warm,
Shadows in gardens, shaded areas doth form,
Slowly disappearing, behind a small passing cloud,
Shade will surround you, like a shroud.

This bright golden ball we yearn to see,
Soon re-appears, above your favorite old tree,
Casting its warmth and light so bright,
A magnificent sight, a perfect delight.

SECTION TEN

ENGLAND

This land in which I was born,
Once ravaged by wars, remains intact, if slightly torn,
Fields of green, in every county abound,
Trees stand tall, magnificently crowned,
Secrets they carry, from times now past,
There future confirmed, as though from a cast,
Waves from the sea, crashing ashore,
Cover beaches used, by rich and poor,
Buildings that rise and reach for the sky,
Styles all varied, no need to ask why,
Cities and towns, live side by side,
Villages still can sometimes hide,
Nature is a wonder, for all to behold,
Caves that are large, dark and cold,
Hills to climb, magnificent sights to be seen,
Places to see, sometimes form a dream,
Castles stand proud, on top of the hills,
Rivers that flow and once served our mills,
Historic houses containing treasure,
There for us to see, at our leisure,
Churches with bells, that ring out loud,
In this my land, of which I am proud,
A place of God's and mans creations,
England my home, there for all, all nations.

– Second Chance –

THE ENGLISH GARDEN

An English garden in summer time,
Sitting there in it's prime,
Flowers in borders, edgings all neatly rimmed,
Lawns mown, perfectly trimmed,
Bright flowers in borders and pots gently swaying,
Children in the distance, happily playing,
Tea and cakes served on the lawn,
Perhaps a game of tennis, teams to be drawn,
Birds in the trees, sweetly singing,
Church bells in the distance, in harmony ringing,
People out walking, in the glorious sun,
Only the children will possibly run,
The wave of a hand, the nod of the head,
A gesture we appreciate, so easily read,
Friends may arrive, enjoy a cool glass of wine,
Laughter rings out, time after time,
Into the dusk, as the sun fades away,
Our time to depart the garden, to prepare for the following day.

– Second Chance –

THE VILLAGE

The sun reflects, on the cool crystal stream,
Winding water flows, just like a dream,
Around the village, finding its way,
Under bridges and roads day by day,
Row's of cottages each side of the road,
Carefully white washed, as if following a code,
Flowers in gardens with colours so bright,
Elegantly standing, in the glorious day light,
Trees standing so bold, some oh so old,
Maintaining there grace, after years in the cold,
The large village green, there for all,
Young and old have answered the call,
To cricket on a sunny summers afternoon,
With tea served in the old pavilion room,
Shops, with roofs of thatch, stand with style and grace,
Quaint small displays, everything has a place,
People will stop, make time for a chat,
Caring and sharing, talking about this and that,
A steep climb is needed to the top of the hill,
Passing gardens growing herbs, like rosemary and dill,
The view from the top, a sight to behold,
Hills, downs and fields, before you like a shower of gold,
The old Norman church, stands proud, large and bold,
Looking over the village now, as in times of old.

– Second Chance –

SPECIAL PLACE

Logs neatly stacked, stand next to the grate,
The glow in the room, slowly fades to the colour of slate,
A fire burns brightly, each flame such a treat,
An invitation to your favorite seat,
Large comfy chairs that once formed a suite,
Stand side by side, so clean and neat,
The rug on the floor absorbing the heat,
A joy to walk on in your bare feet,
Curtains at the window, now fully drawn,
This way they will remain, until way past dawn,
Pictures on the wall, hold memories of the past,
Right next to the door, stands a cabinet so vast,
Rich wooden doors, with handles of brass,
Inside a collection of sparkling glass,
A table stands proud, surrounded by chairs,
Each perfectly matched, forming pairs,
The clock on the mantle now ready to chime,
Ticking away, always showing the right time,
Books on the shelf, ready to read,
This room designed, for your comfort and need.

– Second Chance –

ENGLAND AND WAR

England, blood of so many on your hands,
Spilt in conflict, on land sea and sands,
Men and women who gave their lives, for this their land,
Compassion and sentiment, no where in any plan,
Lives lost, cause hardship and misery for those left behind,
A new way to survive, they have to find,
History tells of wars through out the ages,
Books explain in detail, through out there pages,
Fragile life can be extinguished, with ease,
Prayers un-answered, even their pleas,
Still today men and women go off to fight,
Distant lands still reminded of England's might,
This country which once ruled the world with force,
With mighty army's on foot and horse,
Days long gone, also the power,
Battlefields now green, plants grow and flower,
Memorials erected, commemorate the brave,
These people at peace, as they lay in their grave,
War in the world, part of our every day existence,
Factions demonstrate, show there resistance,
Governments seldom listen, or take note,
Except times, when they covert your vote,
This fragile world, battered and beaten, cries out to live in peace,
Is it not time for hostilities, around the world to cease.

— Second Chance —

WAR

Wars of the past, as wars of today,
Need loyal men and women, to sacrifice their lives the same way,
The detonating bomb, knife or mighty gun,
Can kill in groups, or one by one,
The true cost of war, not domination, power or money, just death,
Blood stained evidence, from people who gasped their last breath.

SECTION ELEVEN

FOUR LEGGED FRIEND

The wag of the tail, the excitement of the bark,
When you arrive home, be it light or dark,
Eyes brightly glowing, slowly melting your heart,
Your four legged friend, from whom you will not part,
Love forms a bond, that keeps you together,
A bond you are aware cannot last forever,
This puppy you choose, so many years ago,
Now a beautiful dog, it's love on you to bestow,
Food and a walk, is all that is required,
Perhaps a cuddle, is so desired,
Laying by the fire, perhaps at your feet,
Relaxed and content, a better friend, so hard to meet,
This dog has a heart and is not just a fashionable trend,
So care and look after your four legged friend.

— Second Chance —

FAITHFUL FRIEND

My faithful friend, how still thou art,
The time now come, when we must part,
Memories race through out my mind,
Of love and affection, that us did bind,
Looks that made my heart beat faster,
I wonder, which one of us really was the master.

– Second Chance –

BIRDS

Look up at the sky, every once in a while,
See birds flying by, with grace and style,
Perfect formations, they can achieve,
Your eyes, will not you deceive,
Flying through the sky, so peaceful, so at ease,
A sight to behold, one to please,
Sometimes they will land, a song they may sing,
Pleasure and joy for all this can bring,
Freely they will just fly away,
Hopefully they will return, another day.

SECTION TWELVE

Other Topics, Including Light Hearted Poetry

THEATRE

The performer on stage now ready to start,
Performing a role, just one small part,
More of the cast will soon appear,
Faces all smiling, some may show fear,
Each one a star, in their own right,
Performances endured by day and night,
The audience, will be the ones who say,
If the show was worth what they had to pay,
The stage is set, there in full swing,
Each song they master as they sing,
Scenery appears with perfect timing,
The show continues, no cracks showing,
Costume changes continue the perfect flow,
A timely cue will instruct you when to rejoin the show,
The performance will end with a magnificent high light,
With costumes usually sparkling and bright,
Applause will ring out, some stand and clap so loud,
For the cast on stage, who have earned the right to feel proud.

— Second Chance —

60'S MUSIC

The sixties saw a massive change,
In popular music, across the range,
New singers appeared, new groups were formed,
A new and exciting style of song was performed,
People in there thousands, stopped and listened,
As a new dawn in music was christened,
But time has progressed,
Some singers, have been laid to rest,
But those magical songs, have survived,
Some have even been revived,
This popular music, still loved by most,
Is played from coast to coast,
Young and old, will dance together,
To this music, I hope will last forever.

– Second Chance –

BOOKS

Books are a treasure, more than just paper and ink,
Past present and future, are the link,
Pages filled with worldly knowledge,
Used to study at schools, university and college.

Books are a treasure, there for all to read,
Questions can be answered, fulfilling a need,
Details revealed, stories to be told,
As the pages slowly unfold.

Books are a treasure, there to read at your leisure,
Bringing you so much pleasure,
Relaxing at home in front of the fire,
A drink by your side if so desired.

Books are a treasure, a gift so great,
The subject of many a debate,
Some now so frail, no one may touch,
From by gone years, from which we have learned so much.

— Second Chance —

CLOCK

The clock on the mantle, slowly ticks away,
Telling the time, day by day,
Proudly it stands for all to see,
Its wooden surround, once part of a tree,
Slowly the hands move round the clock,
Protected by glass and a small brass lock,
This clock passed down, it's age un-known,
Has graced so many a home,
A work of art, so delicate a device,
Once wound always accurate and precise,
The chime on the hour, so delicate, such a delight,
Soft and gentle, both day and night,
An item to cherish and to treasure,
Always around and such a pleasure.

– Second Chance –

REGRET

No I snapped, when offered more tea,
I'm reading can't you see,
My concentration you have disturbed,
For a cup of tea, totally absurd,
I heard that huff, as you walked away,
I will not respond, I have nothing to say,
Once, more I start, to read my book,
Aware of your stare and your angry look,
I will not look up, I have nothing to say,
You were wrong and it will stay that way,
To argue would be a fruitless task,
Over that silly question, you did ask,
At last you leave and your footsteps fade,
Peace and silence, that gesture has made,
Soon I am immersed, back in my story,
Full of treachery, treason, dishonor and glory,
My imagination, takes me to this place,
The characters I meet, face to face,
Disheveled and dirty, clothes all torn,
They fight for their beliefs, the reason they were born,
This belief they never question, but I wonder why,
As in agony they die, underneath a bright blue sky,
The chapter ends, to my own existence, I now return,
My mind suddenly full of remorse and concern,
I know, I must some how make amends,
On this my immediate, happiness depends,
I'll say I'm sorry, in a most sincere way,
Hoping I will not, be made to pay,
For being so rude and so off hand,
To the person on which, I make so many a demand,
Please forgive me, if you can,
I am but a week, feeble man.

— Second Chance —

ALONE

Quietly you listen, for that elusive sound,
A sound that always haunts you, when there's no one around,
It seems to know, when your alone,
Perhaps in your chair, by the phone,
This sound that haunts you, you have never found,
Even though you have searched, all around,
It's hard to describe this sound, that you hear,
Sometimes it makes you shudder, with fear,
But there is no one, in whom you can confide,
No one there, by your side,
Perhaps your phone, will suddenly ring,
Instant joy and happiness, to you, this can bring,
But all too soon, the call will end,
Alone again, on yourself, you must depend,
That sound you know, is on it's way,
It haunts you, night and day,
Through your window, you see the street outside,
People walking by, people you will never meet,
Memories take you back, to days gone by,
Your active life now gone, but why,
You question the decisions, you, yourself once made,
Decisions you now wish, would vanish or fade,
The answers that we seek, we will not always find,
As sometimes what we hear, is deep within our mind.

— Second Chance —

UPPER HAND

Pain, why will you not go away,
There is no way, I want you to stay,
You are with me, everyday,
Even at night, you have your say.

My sins, I gladly confess,
But still, you cause me distress,
I pray each day, that you will go away,
But you just ignore me and stay.

Will I ever again, be free of pain,
My dignity and respect, will I ever regain,
It is hard to explain, or understand,
How much of my body, you demand.

One day perhaps, my pain will go or ease,
Hear my plea, please,
You have been with me, so many years,
Caused me, so many tears.

You always seem, to have the upper hand,
Always the one, in command,
But the time has come, for you to depart,
So my life, I can restart.

– Second Chance –

NURSE

In hospital if you feel unwell,
Rest assured a nurse will attend with a spell,
A potion concocted over many long years,
Inside a syringe, sure to cause you tears,
There smiling faces, only a façade,
Underneath, there mean tough and hard,
Blood they need more often than a vampire,
You cannot protest, this is there empire,
Your bodily functions to a nurse is a pleasure,
If you cannot go, they have a cure, for them a treasure,
Suppositories administered with maximum force,
Sometimes an enema, to them a bigger thrill of course,
Tell them your in pain, this will always make them smile,
Ask for some tablets, the answer, "in a while",
Impossible to sleep day or night,
For they will wake you, "time for temperature and blood pressure all right",
What ever you do never answer back,
They have the upper hand and will pester you just for the crack,
When your time in hospital has come to an end,
They will have driven you around the bend,
There friendly smiling faces can be sadistic,
You could even go as far to say masochistic,
But heed this warning, before hospital and ward you depart,
Give chocolates and a card, this is essential and smart,
This simple gesture will catch them off guard,
Then run for your life as they read the card.

– Second Chance –

SHEET MUSIC

I may be old, so I'm far from young,
My life is a song, now not often sung,
There's many a tale, that I could tell,
If I could speak, or even yell,
My edges are dirty, some slightly torn,
All over you see, I'm very well worn,
The light of the day and that of the night,
Have darkened my pages, so now I'm kept out of sight,
There was a time, when I was in demand,
Full attention, I did command,
Now out of fashion, I've been put away,
In this dark old box, I stay,
But I still remember, those days in the past,
Of hands that were nimble, fingers that were fast,
Music and words, I revealed on every page,
As on the piano I sat and took center stage.

— Second Chance —

KING AND QUEEN

The king and queen sat down to there meal,
Under silver covers, they found jelly with an eel,
Knives and forks in hand, they approached with caution,
Wishing they had been given a smaller portion.

Nervous servants at the table, unable to stand at ease,
Wondering if this delicacy, there majesties would please,
The chief on new ground had decided to tread,
Would the outcome be off with his head.

Their majesties stayed silent as they ate,
Remembering a royal appointment, for which they must not be late,
Smiles appeared, but soon gone from their faces,
Stone cold features replaced smiles with no traces.

They had to act and speak with care,
There destination, served this traditional fare,
The elephant and castle, is where they can be seen,
This there first ever venue, as the purley King and Queen.

— Second Chance —

TIME FOR TEA

Now friends I invited, round for tea,
Best china used, for all to see,
The table dressed, with a cloth of pure white,
Placed by the window to catch the light,
Chairs arranged, for all to have a seat,
The room cleaned, everything tidy and neat,
Cakes and sandwiches, I did prepare,
A feast for all to share,
Everything in place, another check I did make,
Wondering if enough cakes, I did bake,
No time to worry, I must get ready,
People will soon arrive, my nerves I must keep steady,
A final check, ensured a perfect display,
Now no one arrived, to my dismay,
So on the phone I got, to have my say,
But oh how silly I felt when told, I had said the following day.

— Second Chance —

WISDOM

I met this man, he told me he was going to the fair,
He bid me well, but told me to take care,
Why is that so, I asked of him,
My brother he said, his face so grim,
Danger does lurk where ever you tread,
Through hills and valleys, even amongst the dead,
His hand he rested on my shoulder,
Told me his wisdom was because he was older,
Bade me fare well, then was on his way,
A curious occurrence, thought I this fine day,
His words ringing in my mind,
Could ever again, I trust man kind,
Now many people I passed along the road,
Not stopping, his words echoing like a code,
My destination I finally did reach,
To purchase some fruit, especially a peach,
My wallet from my pocket was needed to pay,
It was not there, I did not know what to say,
Other pockets I did check, to no avail,
My face now drained, became pale,
Those words were not of wisdom, I was his prey,
Into his trap I walked, another victim this fine day.

– Second Chance –

MEANS

I once knew a man, his name was Mark,
Energetic, a real bright spark,
He squandered his money each and every day,
Extravagant life style, way above his pay,
He laughed and joked, even when he was broke,
When his money was gone he stayed home, drank coke,
So called friends, now no where to be found,
At least he had his faithful old hound,
With debts out of control and still mounting,
The pennies he had to start counting,
Credit with held, instructions from his bank,
Now he certainly felt his lower rank,
Expenditure now brutally pruned back,
He must ensure he does not get the sack,
This his life style for many long years,
A time he dreads and fears,
The lesson in life, is to live with in your means,
The rest you can have, but only in your dreams.

— Second Chance —

BACK

Oh my back, here we go again,
Now I will have to cancel, my trip to Spain,
This pain you inflict on me, with ease,
Is guaranteed to annoy, not please,
I keep you warm, treat you with respect,
Not once can I remember, when you I did neglect,
You cripple me, with every move I make,
One day my revenge on you I will take,
Walking stick in hand, I slowly make my way,
Longing for the day when I will make you pay,
You have the upper hand at this present time,
Rest assured, I will make you pay for this crime.

– Second Chance –

CHRISTMAS PREPARATIONS

People rushing all around,
That elusive present, to be found,
Shops brightly lit, entice you in,
Your custom hoping to win,
Time you make from your work load so great,
Even though you have more than enough on your plate,

Rain shine, sleet or snow,
This task you must do, even if you are low,
Time passes at an alarming pace,
More and more people, now joining this race,
Homes to clean, food to prepare,
Can bring you to the edge of despair,

Presents must be hidden, time found to decorate the tree,
To sparkle away for all to see,
Excited children, perform there school play,
More time from your busy day,
Shopping for food at this time of year,
No room to move, everything so dear,

Cards posted, some still to write,
More time to find, perhaps late at night,
Presents to deliver and hide, as more arrive,
The day fast approaches, children elated, so alive,
Final preparations now in place,
Presents under the tree, placed with style and grace,

Second Chance

Sacks filled, brightly coloured paper showing,
Ribbons and bows with glitter glowing,
At last Christmas morn has arrived,
Your spirits, you can revive,
Happiness, laughter and cheer,
Repay your dedication, as in this moment you all share.

— Second Chance —

CHRISTMAS EVE

Festive homes, stand against a back drop so stark,
Twinkling lights, in windows sparkle in the dark,
Excitement abundant in so many homes,
Decorated trees of traditional green to modern chrome,
Stockings hang on fire places and beds,
Different colours, but mostly reds,
Mince pies left out for Santa Clause,
Will he have time to stop and pause,
So many homes for him to visit this Christmas Eve,
He will be here, as the children in him believe.

— Second Chance —

TURKEY

The man that feeds us is coming along,
Singing that same ridiculous old song,
He trying his best to fatten each and every one of us,
We know his game, but will cause no fuss,
He has no idea, we are all on a diet,
Getting ready for the first ever Christmas Turkey riot.

– Second Chance –

DREAM

Oh land far away,
One day with you I will stay,
To sample the treasures, that you gladly give,
To embrace your warmth, as each day I live,
To run my fingers, through your soil,
Where men and women, once did toil,
To learn your history and to understand,
To enjoy each day, but on you make no demand,
Like waves from the sea, that come gently ashore,
Each one as different, as the one before,
The sun enjoyed, in the sky each day,
Shines brighter as to you, it makes its way,
Oh land far away,
How I long for this day,
When my dreams, will finally come true,
And I can walk in your embrace, under your beautiful sky of blue.

– *Second Chance* –

TO THE END

The true gift of life, will it ever be known,
Grown from seeds, man hath sown,
This world is our home, on which we depend,
As we journey on, to our life's end.